Generation Txt

Edited by Tom Chivers

Born 1983, Tom Chivers is an energetic writer, editor and promoter of poetry. His creative and critical work has been published in *Stride*, *Fire*, *The Libertine*, *Culture Wars*, *CEN*, *Babylon Burning: 9/11 Five Years On*, *nthposition*, *Tears in the Fence* and elsewhere. His first collection is forthcoming in Spring 2007. Tom is Director of penned in the margins, producing innovative live literature events and tours, publishing new work and representing spoken word artists. He presents London's only weekly radio show devoted to contemporary poetry on Resonance 104.4FM. For more information please visit www.pennedinthemargins.co.uk

GENERATION TXT

Joe Dunthorne
Inua Ellams
Laura Forman
Emma McGordon
Abigail Oborne
James Wilkes

**penned in
the margins**
publishing

PUBLISHED BY PENNED IN THE MARGINS
53 Arcadia Court, 45 Old Castle Street, London E1 7NY
www.pennedinthemargins.co.uk

First edition published 2006
Second edition published 2007

Printed in Great Britain by the MPG Books Group, Bodmin and King's Lynn

ISBN
0-9553846-1-3
978-0-9553846-1-5

The editor would like to thank the following people for their assistance in bringing Generation Txt to life: Sarah Dustagheer, Rob at Biddles, Kevin Ward.

Contents

Introduction   ix

JOE DUNTHORNE
Eating Out   1
Rubens' paintings at the National Gallery   3
I made a grown woman cry last night   4
Quite intelligent pigs   5
Sean's stapler is a castanet   6
Advice for red balloons   7
Sestina for my friends   8
Taking a photo of workmen in Chapelfield gardens   10

INUA ELLAMS
Kissed by a Rose   13
Epic   17
For the fighters and lovers   19
Lizards and Lollypop Sticks   23

LAURA FORMAN
For sale   27
Static   28
Prognosis   29
Watchman   30
Sunday shoes   31
Attention   32
Picnic   33
Redeveloping Battersea   34

EMMA MCGORDON
Punks & Patchouli   37
Sonnet to the Soviet   39
The Scary Thing About Those Who Jump   40
The System   42
Hecate's Silver   44
Sexy Anne's Plan   46
Love Letters   48

ABIGAIL OBORNE
suffering   51
Kid   52
Poems   53
sonnet no.3   54
sonnet no.11   55
sonnet no.13   56
The World   57
coz I'm   58
Sunday Ten to Three   60

JAMES WILKES
Ex Chaos   63
Score for a Nocturne   64
Untitled   65
A postcard from the New Forest   66
A postcard from Rochester   67
A postcard from the Isle of Purbeck   68
A postcard from Eldon Hole   69
Tea   70
4 variations on the same midwinter   73
Wild Flowers of Britain and Europe   74

Generation Txt

INTRODUCTION

'I started writing when I was 28. I don't think people
really write anything worth reading before that.'
Kate Clanchy, *The Daily Telegraph*, 13 March 2004

One can only presume that Ms Clanchy would make exceptions
for Keats, Wordsworth, Rimbaud and Wilfred Owen; Coleridge,
Chatterton, Hart Crane and Sylvia Plath. Not to mention the winners of
the Foyle Young Poets of the Year Award 2006 of which Clanchy was
a judge. Because all of these poets - and many more besides - wrote
some of their best work years before their twenty-eighth birthday.

Poetry is a craft and, yes, craft takes time. But when new writing talent
is ignored or, at worst, deliberately suppressed, you know something's
up. There are some positive initiatives within the British poetry scene
such as the *Reactions* anthologies and the Foyle and Eric Gregory
Awards, but there remains a general unwillingness amongst some in
the 'industry' to engage seriously with young writers.

Generation Txt is an attempt to redress the balance, to give some of
our most talented and promising young writers a platform for their
work. From over one hundred and fifty submissions from all over
the UK we've found six poets in their early and mid- twenties, six
of the best. This is the generation that reached adulthood either side
of the Millennium, the generation of Blogs, iPods and ASBOs; the
generation of 9/11 and 7/7.

Louis Simpson of *Harvard Review* called poetry 'the struggle to
express the contemporary'. The poems in this anthology are up to
that challenge, tackling modern life head on. From gun crime and
teenage tearaways in Inua Ellams' work to the surreal office comedy
of Joe Dunthorne's 'Sean's stapler is a castanet'. This is undeniably
contemporary poetry.

Young writers are often encouraged to 'find their own voice', a
poetic register sufficiently mature to be independent of its influences.

You'll find here a wide range of voices in development that reflect the diversity of contemporary writing practice. A concern for representing everyday language - a practice with countless forerunners, from Chaucer through Gerard Manley Hopkins to the Black Mountain poets - is present in much of the work. Abigail Oborne is particularly adept at capturing the fractured syntax of modern speech.

> I'm sick of like,
> listening to
> but sorry's a funny word
> stop being such a retard
> or
> in the here and now and
> getting sick of whinging
>   ('Poems')

And Laura Forman's opening poem brilliantly parodies the marketing-speak of duplicitous estate agents.

> Studio flat, quiet location, no chain.
> Underground heating or air conditioning
> According to the choices you've made.
> External walls with polished hardwood veneers
> To suit other people's taste.
>   ('For Sale')

Laura works as a copy writer so is in the right place to understand the ways in which language can be used - *and abused*. Indeed, the writers in this anthology are constantly alert to the power and possibilities of poetry as an urgent, dynamic artform. Inua Ellams fuses hip-hop and beat rhythms with a kind of high lyricism reminiscent of the Romantics, declaiming 'I am the sum of all things / non-factual'. Emma McGordon's work is often startling and is underlaid with a subtle but definite political anger (something she shares with her former mentor, the late Barry MacSweeney). Dorset-born James Wilkes offers a dissenting voice against the decline of the countryside.

> Countryside's only good for

Burning onions, anyway, cover it
In slush of brine and
Teleport the inhabitants to Saudi.
                    ('Wild Flowers of Britain and Europe')

Elsewhere his work is defined by its formal restraint, an economy of expression we associate with Modernist poetics. With a degree in Philosophy and a background in visual art, James is the most consciously experimental of the writers here, challenging the reader to plot his or her own path through a rich but slippery text. We include here some of his 'postcard-poems' that rework selections of writing by Daniel Defoe.

James Wilkes is a creator of physical 'poem objects' and he is not alone in confronting the clichéd image of the writer labouring in his garret, isolated from the real world. Joe Dunthorne and Inua Ellams are both regular performers at literature and music festivals, whilst Emma McGordon works as a freelance writer and workshop leader in prisons and schools in her native Cumbria, and has been Poet in Residence at Alnwick Garden Centre, Northumberland.

This is an exciting time for poetry, with new opportunities for writers to perform, educate and collaborate with other artists. And the internet is providing new ways to publish and promote poetry. Which is probably a good place to plug www.myspace.com/generationtxt

Because *Generation Txt* wouldn't be complete without a MySpace account. So log on, be our friend and keep up-to-date with our forthcoming national live poetry tour.

In the meantime, I hope you find poems in this anthology that inspire, entertain and make you think. Above all, poems that follow Ezra Pound's command and 'Make it new'.

Tom Chivers
East London, December 2006

JOE DUNTHORNE

Joe graduated from the Creative Writing Prose MA at the University of East Anglia, where he was awarded the Curtis Brown Prize. In 2005 he travelled to Bangladesh with the British Council as part of an exchange project with young Bangladeshi writers. He is currently an associate lecturer in Creative Writing at the Open University. His poetry has been featured on Channel 4 and published in some magazines, and he has recently completed his first novel, *Submarine*. Joe is twenty-four years old and based in London.

Eating Out

There are dumpsters simply brimming
with left overs and send backs,
black sacks full of nummy slop:
coconut pannacotta
truffle honey mozzarella
California bouillabaisse
and even if you mush
the food together
I'll bet it still tastes pretty good
but then, you see,
there are these down-by-luck
table-salt of the earth types:
smelling like asparagus piss,
no money, no grub,
little half-healed cuts on their nose bridges,
and anyhow
you'd think they might be allowed
to lick a strand of marinated pig fat
from the inside of a bin bag
but no, because the nosh,
even when it's been tossed out,

1

still represents the chef
– it's still product –
and they say a restaurant's reputation
is only equal to its clientele
and, on occasion, these homeless chaps
shout abuse through letter boxes
so the really good restaurants
have a cage,
a big steel cage in the alley out the back,
to protect the scraps
from these poor sods
with their bellies cramping
and their sunburnt eyelids
and so, I mean,
it makes you feel terribly helpless really,
forty slightly overdone scallops
going to rot in a cage, imagine.

Rubens' paintings at the National Gallery

It's like a mosh pit, says the girl with the blue-striped tights
observing Perseus: he straddles tens of ham-thighed
soldiers, holding Medusa's head at arms-length,
eyes averted, appalled by her try-hard haircut.
She's long dead but her dread look still yucks plenty:
spears halt in the freshly cemented grips of sure-to-fail minions.

Rubens milks filth from the bib-heavy maid's basket
of fruit. No ambiguity here as the hand of a cad
with a *ya-know-ya-would* smirk parts the labia
of a clit-stoned fig. I'm thinking *Viz*. A billboard-sized
canvass depicts stacks of darkened carcasses:
one way to suggest his penchant for fucking.

The gallery tongues click. An eight-year-old checking
out Constable with his hands down his pants
announces: *wonderful, simply wonderful.*

I made a grown woman cry last night

I made a grown woman cry last night.
I was seven times her size.
I told her she had lost her looks.
I said her heart was all gristle
and her lungs, rolled-up cereal packets.
I said her spine was collapsible
like a telescope,
I said, like a telescope I can see into your past.
Your husband left you even though
you did nothing wrong in particular
it was just like – Christ – I'm so fucking bored.
I made a grown woman cry last night.
I was fifteen times her size.
Meg Ryan, Meg Ryan, Meg Ryan – the woman
your husband is with looks a bit like Meg Ryan.

Quite intelligent pigs

I remember when Carmel,
my wife's pet pig,
showed great ingenuity
in digging a tunnel
to break out of her pen.
She even found the house key
that was hidden
beneath the plant pot
and ransacked our trot-in-wardrobe.
Later that day I spotted her,
trying to snuffle past the bouncer
outside The Barony Pub,
all trussed up in an Ascot hat,
two pairs of heels,
smelling of Gaultier and swill.

After my wife left me,
I couldn't bear to keep Carmel.
They learn to mimic their owners
and the memories were too painful.
I hung her from the gambrel, split
from neck to belly like an unzipped
jacket, dripping into a bucket,
singing badly about the way it hurt.
She sold well at Tavistock market
– chitterlings, chaps,
loin chops, the lot –
but I still can't shake the memory
of my wife's barrow expression
after I caught her, trough-deep,
in a shepherd's crotch.

Sean's stapler is a castanet

"Jellyfish gurgle through the watercooler," says Sean
who works for the foreign rights department.
He cannot stop using his imagination.

"Must have run out of kryptonite," he says, when the Xerox machine
breaks. Colleagues blame problems in his home-life. "Translucent
jellyfish gurgle through the watercooler," says Sean.

He still has friends. Sam says: "Take a week off, go for some
walks, get it out of your system." "I haven't got a system," he laments,
"I cannot stop using my imagination."

Mr. Grist invites him for an informal chat: "You seem withdrawn;
what's been getting to you?" "I'm worried about the environment;
Jellyfish gurgle through the watercooler," says Sean.

Sean forgets his quarterly review. Mr. Grist finds him shredding paper,
                                                            having fun
with Eighties wigs, bird nests, pompoms. Sean adopts a Dutch accent:
"I cannot shtop u-shing my imaginashun."

His colleagues organise a farewell party at the aquarium.
Wearing T-shirts bearing his slogans, they perform a re-enactment:
"Jellyfish gurgle through the watercooler," says Sam,
"I cannot stop using my imagination."

Advice for red balloons

Rise above the Roman Catholic Cathedral
then push past the balconies
of the waffle-stack estate.
Skim the dried-out flowers,
they are green and yellow.
Hang outside the YMCA
until you are attracted by a boy
whose hair stands on end.
Let him tie an envelope
to your tail, addressed to Caroline.

Sail with it, along the railway
tracks, and as the fields
turn yellow and green
you'll see them, slap-handed
against the windows
of standard class carriages
with notions of treasure maps,
party invites, scratch cards,
hard cash, a large ornate key,
a list of miscellaneous
phone numbers, tickets
for Santana, that new car smell,
sex-desperate postcards
from lonely, coastal women
as you dangle on, semi-translucent,
just below the power lines.

Sestina for my friends

I know what my friends think
of me because of the things they say:
"Joe, you are shiny and worthwhile and always
thinking of others." I am not so great.
I could name at least five people who are better,
overall. Here's one of my faults: I'm forever calculating

how to present myself in any given situation. Calculating
people give W.G. Sebald's *Rings of Saturn* as a gift, and think
that the person receiving the book will think better
of them. After reading it they will say:
"Joe – it was beautiful, I mean, he's like the great
gramps I never had. He even made Suffolk compelling." I always

give *Rings of Saturn* as a gift, sometimes even to boys. *Always*
is too much. I have given it twice, if I'm calculating
honestly. Once to a girl who thought I was great
for just over a month until she suspected, correctly, that I think
I am more interesting than her. If I say
that the boy I gave it to was far better

at football than me, then I think you understand. Better
to be left for dead on the right wing, always
knowing that the boy who embarrassed you – let's say
his name is Luke – has this book in his bedroom. I'm calculating
that he won't have sold it because he thinks,
nay *hopes* that one day he might read it, this great

and clever book that was a gift from a friend who is not great
at football but by God, he's got a brain and, ultimately, it's better
to have enormous thoughts than to be almost semi-pro. I think
that great people do not have these sorts of thoughts. I always
keep my mauled copy somewhere half-inconspicuous, calculating
the sort of spot where guests will see it, sure, but they will not say

I bet Joe put that there so I see it. More likely, they'll say,

huh, such a clever book, just lying by his football boots. It's great
to know someone like Joe who's clever but doesn't rub your face in it.
                                                    Calculating
people are some of the worst people in existence. This poem is better
for its honesty. Even when I admit this stuff, my friends can always
fall back on my honesty. He thinks

too much, they think. We'd best not say
anything about that sestina. To us, he'll always be great,
better than great, more like excellent. Or this is what I'm calculating.

Taking a photo of workmen in Chapelfield gardens

I wanted to take a picture of these four workmen;
they wore high-visibility vests that said Ardmore
on the back. Three of them were sat on a bench,
facing the pagoda; they had the sort of haircuts
that let you see the shape of their skulls.
The fourth man was having a rest, laid out
on the path, eyes scrunched against the sun.
I was lying on the grass behind them. The symmetry
was perfect: the pagoda in frame, Ardmore
Ardmore Ardmore, green and yellow flowers,
a man sleeping at brunch-time.
I lifted my camera and, immediately,
the man woke up and asked if I had a problem.
I said: "No, mate," which was a bit of an assumption.
He came over to speak to me; his colleagues looked over
their shoulders to watch. He had his hard hat under his arm.
I tried to explain about the symmetry
and the perfection of tired men
and that he was lying on the floor
like some Fifties starlet on top of a grand piano.
I told him about the old world charm of the pagoda,
cans of Super Tennants on the bandstand.
"It just seemed to me to be beautiful," I said.
"You were beautiful."
"You should have asked," he said.
"Sorry," putting my camera away. "Sorry."
But he still had the sun in his eyes
and I had my notebook with me.

Inua Ellams

Inua's first love was graphic art. The first time he toyed with a pen he immediately fell in love with the magic line that grew from the point that touched the paper. Citing Shakespeare, Keats, MosDef and Talib Kweli as influences, Inua has performed at numerous venues including Tate Britain, RADA, The Drum, The Albany Theatre, Glastonbury and Latitude Festivals and at distinguished street corners across the world. His first pamphlet of poems, *Thirteen Fairy Negro Tales*, was released in 2005 by Flipped Eye Publishing. Inua is twenty-two years old, lives in South London and believes in aPple jUice.

Kissed by a Rose

I am from the abyss.
I am from the crater caused
when earth last French-kissed the sun
I am the sum of all things
non-factual, I am the actual son
of a defunct Osirus
drunk on rum
lost in the darkness of faded perceptions
riding jaded redemption songs
through neon braided wildernesses
toking sess to smoke signals of:
'Help, hope wanted here'...

There I stood
arms stretched
fingers filtering space
hoping to catch comets
to trace fire-ribbons around
the embers of my being
and reignite me back to life.

But I have been soaked
in a bucket of bad luck
then locked
in a chastity belt
frozen in an iceberg
soldered to a bomb
hung to near death
forced to drink
poison from a glass
sending me spinning
gasping to the road sides
of a dead emotion
of no motion
no light
no love
and my limbs spread-eagle
across a gaping black hole
lashed with an endless hiss
spewing form the mouth of it

and I am from there,

I am from that abyss
Dancing blue toed and bare footed
on a knife's edge, life force amiss
like a burning orchestra
making a last stand
cursed with turntables
blasting 'bling' 'bling'
through the dying echoes
of a symphony of keeping-it-realness
with a gun totting time, hanging
like a backcloth to the stage-tragedy
of my life, writing with world's weight
on my pen, reason run rife
sails at half mast
reaching breaking point

tension rising
to the back drop of all this
I met you.

I met you.

And in the silent seconds it took
for that reason to re-root itself
in nothing.

In the stretch of a smile
in the moment of a moment
in the Birth of breath,
in the short contact of skin
soaked in feathers,
dawn broke…

Like silhouetted secrets,
tipped with gold,
glazing like laid-back-lakes
through solid boulders
emerging like a god's shoulder
for me to cry on
effervescent
misty
like a satisfactory sigh
like a mystic on acid-
freeloading of divinity
like whoa!
like whispers through pillows
like wading through a cloud's caress
like yes
like no
like yes
like effortless
like effortlessly

You became the light

on the dark side of me.

So here I sit
cross legged on the lawns
of your soul, my spirit soaring
six feet above me
eyes closed
right cheek chosen
to bear the gift
of a glass-slipper-like-lip-print
of a last kiss
frozen within it
and my heart glowing
three shades of gold
I neither know the consequence
or the cause

all I know is

I have been kissed

by a rose

on the grey

Epic

she is a lady at a train station
soul swaying from side to side
sprit tap dancing day dreams
and dandelions around her.
Body stands still, eyes closed
hair whispering to wind
Brixton in her back pack.

He is a suit in awe of swaying and dancing
dandelions day-ing through eyes closed
hair whispering to wind
Camden in his knapsack.

Together they are a picture perfect
pasted in a train station, palms pressed
together like pilgrims praying.
They synchronise their swaying
in a hug, and instantly become more,

they embrace like two dying stars twisting
in the twilight, turning, trailing swaying…
they part briefly, hearts waning   and kiss.
In a flash flutter flip bliss
they become even more,

two soaring stars swaying,
two supernovas in a train station, staining
as light lances through tunnels taming shadows
shaming all. At the peak of lips locked together
they part, fall, and depart
like lilies after a snow's fall.

- - - - -

And I know a lady that leaves like that.
She has lilies for lips and when we kiss, it feels like nectar
and my guilt is chasing flowers. For then, between her lips
I morph to them: the floating fractals on the wings
of fauna, fore playing between her petals
fading to nothing when we stop.

Then I-sighs rise, exhaling, swaying,
cumulous cloud quaking, climbing

in moments like this of unwinding
love lays its first foot prints, finding
foot holds in lips printing
promises, paving paths
like the palms of pilgrims playing
two pairs of petals swaying
two pairs of lips locked in like-making
two stories
two heart
beats one kiss

one moment

epic

For the fighters and lovers

When dawn breaks
like a stretched sonata silence
brown handling the fantastic blue,
When dust litters the new quite
like the substance of prophecies
before the periods of bloom
and life lulls the living back
to the true paths of life

Our change will come.

It will come
after a tumultus multitude
of fighters have expired for a reason
not worth the breath it is uttered with.

It will come
after the structures of global lies fall
sparking that Exodus
movement of the people
with their minds in tow;
it will come.

Then those born
by the river will gather around
camp fires and finally stop running.
The metronomic but melodious humming
of tired mothers will reach a crescendo
and pause.
Sailors will let up their oars
and let the current take them theirs.
The powers of imagination
will be fully revealed to men
and they will exactly who they are
and who they can be.

This will set us free;
free falling towards a second
of sensory sovereignty
as our senses go insane.

That moment will taste,
like a teaspoon full
of forbidden fruit shake.

Mixed with Lotus water
and lugubriously ladled
onto a parched tongue
till the whole mouths
is rendered rhapsodic
reeling with intent
wonder and hope.

It will smell
like fresh pharaohs of the new sun
ancient and young,
like old wisdom riding a BMX
between freight trains
in a freezing rain
stained with child's play
and laughter.

Then after
it will sound
like a cello made of rosewood
exhaling soft poetry
over a brown village at night
in the quite after the tempest goes
making the atmosphere finally feel good.

and it will feel
like a hug
from God.

Finished with a squeeze
saying "your time has come".

And then our time will come.

Our suffering
will be the greatest stories ever told.
Symbols of our heartache
will be treasured in sacred places
as constant reminders
that Love never fails,
never folds.

Our tears will be recognized as rain clouds
and they will be danced beneath,
this will be a reflex, uncharted, untold,
And our silences will be reincarnated as light,
after years of just being golden.

This is not Fantasy;
this is reality
with a dream complex.

I have seen it written in old books,
it is the subject of Negro spirituals,
it has been spoken of by those
that have trespassed in paradise
and returned whole.

This is our destiny
and we are destined to reach that goal.
Though weeping may endure for the night
joy comes in the morning
and as we suffer
we gain the passage right
so hold on to the tempest
and never let go
stay strong

hold on
hold tight

Lizards and Lollypop Sticks

I was once told
that when the sun shines
and the rain falls
a Lion is born.

That day was brilliant.
Blue was the sky and beneath it,
I skimmed the red clay
of my father's courtyard, high on lollypops

tormenting lizards with sticks and stones
dyed in childhood mischief
straight from the bone.
But in a bullet's blink,

through the refined sunrays
rain clouds rolled in, sky dams burst
Bisons, Boars, Beasts!
I heard the new born King roar.

And though I rear
no regard for royalty
my reaction was predestined
I danced.

I jumped whooped and hollered
like a tap dog un-collared
like Crazy Legs was African
dancing to 'Ice-rap's valediction

I danced like tomorrow was fiction.
Hell,
tomorrow IS fiction
'now' is a valediction to todays gone before

that tapers on time like tapestries of memories

moored on mortal matter, bleeding to breeze.
Formed of the ill fated fabric of dreams
their substance be their flattered flaws.

But my dance was flawless.
Call me an outlaw cause
I romanced that rain rhythm
like my middle name was 'Lawless'.

I jived like that last disciple of Neptune
jiving till talk of me spread
through the Mermaids and Mami waters.
They heard that a slave to H20, moon-slid

blood diamonds from melting crystals
and sowed them in stalks of time
through tap's tones.
Yet, I was not alone.

My lone reign-ing was long flown.
Bare feet slapped on concrete
bred ghost like visions etched in bone
raised through marrowed mirrors

the sparrow sings straight
that some have danced now before.
And before my very rhythm,
Rain splash revealed those rift riders hidden:

nine numinous nether Nigerian heroes
that bounced bodegas out of colonial battle grounds
to the beat of never ending "NO"s.
They make Iyanga to the sun

and freestyle freedom
feeding on Jollof rice
mangoes, melanin
and moonlight.

Together, we danced
like this was right and eternity was wrong
like Egwugwu masqueraded as humans
forming forefather fever, feet foaming…

And as sudden as the rain came
as quickly as dark cotton perforated the sun
those rain clouds were gone
And all that remained

was vapours rising, garments wet
and the lizards and lollypop sticks
that witnessed the fitness
of a summer's shower power

a lion being born
and a barefooted Brown Viking
who danced fiction
out of form.

'Iyanga' is a word from a Nigerian language meaning to 'show off '.

An 'Egwugwu' is a from the same language. Essentially, it is a man dressed up in a wild ceremonial attire, who when dressed like this, was believed to represent one of the ancestral spirits of the land.

LAURA FORMAN

Twenty-seven year old Laura's poems have been published in *The North*, *Smiths Knoll*, *The Interpreter's House* and *iota*. A 'poem poster' designed by MadeThought was exhibited at the British Library. She has written a short story inspired by the Circle Line for *From Here to Here* and an essay on Patrick Hamilton for *Common Ground*. After graduating from Cambridge University, Laura hung up her lab coat and moved to London to work for a brand consultancy. After five years of naming, slogans and tone of voice projects she moved on to become copy manager at John Lewis. Laura is now fluent in the language of haberdashery, large electrical appliances and much more besides. She blogs about her foodie adventures at urbanberry.blogspot.com

For sale

Studio flat, quiet location, no chain.
Underground heating or air conditioning
According to the choices you've made.
External walls with polished hardwood veneers
To suit other people's taste.
Screw-down security door.
No need to be close to local amenities.
Ideal for last-time buyers.
Available sooner than you think.

Static

Okay. Hungerford Bridge is the numbery strip
On an old-fashioned radio and I'm
The plasticy bit that moves along it.
Starting out without really thinking,
Computer-numb from work. Sheeny dark –
Pupils grow from the full stops
Fluorescent office-whiteness demands.

Ignore Charing Cross rattling its trains:
Just the burst of noise as I tune out of
A station. Keep going. Got to get through the frequencies
Of this couple's Early Evening Showdown and this lot's
On the Way to the Theatre with Friends programme.
Big Ben chimes and it's time. Forehead lines
With the effort of the Whether-it's-true-Report.
Do you read me? Do you read me?

Prognosis

They sewed it shut.
Pulled the edges together with those stitches
that seem too industrial, too thick
to persuade cells, barely introduced,
to hold on to each other through the night.

Interesting plan. But not completely watertight.
At least, not at first.
Each morning, how many people
scraped ageing marmalade pots
without thinking to compare the bits round the edge
with that weirdly crystalline ooze you leaked?

But you got a bit better each day. It was like
one of those soap operas where nothing seems to happen
in any given episode but if you look back one month, two, six,
you can count three divorces, a marriage,
two births, eleven crimes and a terminal disease.

So here we are. Wondering if they got it all.
I put my finger to your scar.
I have to hush it, keep it quiet.

Watchman

Escaping the TruBrite bleached-teeth white of the supermarket,
I sliptoe over gothic-greasy scales growing
On this slumber-heavy cobblemonster's back.
Its digestive systems rumble underfoot
With shifts of partially digested commuters.

Monday night so I've five-a-day times four to last the week.
Puzzled citrus bright immigrants shiver in my plastic bags.
I ignore the respiratory health of the entire globe for a
Tonguetwist of vitamins from jetset fruits.

Feet press leaves into wet stains on pavements.
The slowed swing of headlights
Makes sequins of drizzledrops on cellophane
Quivering round pointless flowers I'll give to my
Silent evening, waiting eye-to-spyhole, behind the front door.

Sunday shoes

When my mum does it,
It is pair by pair,
On a need to wear basis.
A quick blast of Sparkle
And a rub with a cloth
Like the old days of licking a hanky.

But when my dad does it,
He summons them all from unseen places.
Calls them from the bottom of the stairs
To see if they'll stand on their own two feet.

They're lined up in colours.
It looks as if our feet have
Shed their skin
Again and again.

He's the mayor of the garage,
Inspecting rows of the clean and shiny,
Stopping to buff the scuffs
Of Monday to Saturday.

I can see his face in them.

Attention

You let me abseil down your forehead.
I dived off your nose, went potholing in facial pores,
tried trampolining on an eardrum.

I flew stunt kites in your sighs,
teetered over balance beam collarbones,
ski-ed the moguls of your ribs,
staged a swimming display in your bellybutton.

A pubic hair stood in for a bungee rope.
I clung to your kneecap,
one bruised arm aloft for the rodeo.
I excelled myself on the parallel bars of your toes.
You hardly felt a thing.

Picnic

The sky was up early today,
Scrubbing away last night's stars
With summer soap and an old, thin cloud
For a healthy blue glow.

Looks like the sun's lazing at home.
Can't be bothered to fly off for a long weekend.
It's pottering around in a park near my flat.
We'll head there too.

I'm rifling through cupboards, aiming
Ingredients at Tupperware targets,
Scanning the shelves with metal detector eyes
That quiver when they find a treasure.

I build an igloo in my rucksack.
Sandwich box, cool block, sandwich box, cool block
And prepare for the trek up the hill to meet you.
Huskies run away from my fear-laden sled.

You're waiting at the summit,
The flag of your impatience flies in my face.
Beer skitters over the glacier in my throat.
My stories are frozen.

Lounging on ice-sharpened blades of grass,
I listen the to tick of a dandelion clock.
You pick it. It's the skeleton of a spent firework
But we'll catch our death in its avalanche.

Redeveloping Battersea

As we know from the principle of conservation,
Energy cannot be created or destroyed. So they're transforming
This unreal estate into a cultural powerhouse.
It's been in a state of flux for years.
The potential difference to the surrounding area is generating
A real buzz. Executive flats are being snagged as we speak
And the infinity pool is very nearly complete.
So this, the current project, is the one they're plugging.
Patrons will be able to enjoy pre-performance beverages
While a lone soprano snakes up and down arpeggios
And critics sharpen their pencils – all hoping
For that truly electric atmosphere. But they won't have heard
The whirring loss of purpose or the broken sound
Of someone standing quiet in the ruin, one heart humming.

Emma McGordon

Emma McGordon was born and raised in Whitehaven, West Cumbria. She began writing poetry at school and met the late poet Barry MacSweeney at a writers' group when she was 15. Her first pamphlet collection, *The Hangman and the Stars*, was published by his Blacksuede Boot Press when she was 17. Emma was Northern Young Writer of the Year 2002 and is currently poet-in-residence at Alnwick Garden Centre, Northumberland. She returned to her native Cumbria in 2005 after training to be a journalist in Newcastle and studying English Literature at the University of Liverpool.

Punks & Patchouli

And the smell of un-dusted
Houses.
    Purple curtains
Black leather jacket,
        socks
Pulled over your skinny-fit
        Jean.

Eye-shadow seen
    Only through a cloudy haze
Of roll-your-own smoke.

Punks & Patchouli.

Waiting in shop door way

For a bus
        Or a lift
        Or somebody

On a motorbike.

Somebody who rides
With a spare helmet tucked
                    beneath his arm

that's what she'd like.

Sonnet to the Soviet

In memory of Irina Rostovtseva

I did not meet her at the town bus stop,
But I dreamt of her strong forehead nightly,
Her make-blood-run-cold stare, her sprightly hair
And the shape of her fingertips. Mop my
Brow and fear to think of how she strummed
A guitar so hard the strings were bloody,
Stalin's boots caked with it. The muddy dead
Heard no musik. Still the flies hummed low.

She was a non-party member from Moscow,
They found her with a full cup but no saucer,
An experiment with closer inspection.
Revealing her a scientist.Looks like show time
For men with guns. 1922 she was born
Shot 20th / 50. Charge: Unknown.

The Scary Thing About Those Who Jump

The scary thing about somebody
Jumping from the top of a tall building
Is not the fall or the jump itself
Or the rush of air that chokes
Into being that person's last breath.
It is not even the man, on his way to work,
Who finds the seven body parts
Spread across six paving stones.
It is not the sirens that are blue
With nothing to rush to,
Nor the cold of the zipper on and a black
Silver body bag,
Or the sound of the bristles
That are pushed forth and back
Forth and back
Until nobody would know of the life
That once saw its last there.

The scary thing about somebody
Jumping from the top of a tall building
Is the dark that they saw when
They stood on the ledge and
Looked for the stars.
It is maybe that they took the stairs
Two at a time,
Or the pile of rubbish they saw
Swirling in circles too small
To catch the headlines of that day's
News report.
It is the town that was deserted
And that nobody saw them walk
Through the streets or stand at the foot
Of the building
And look up.
It is the look on their face as they chose
Which coat to wear

And it is the way they closed their blue front door
Knowing that they had no need to take a key.

The System

The traffic lights are on red
Yet still the pedestrian stands still,
Choked and drugged up
On life's non-moving, un-decision
Insecurity pill.

From a broken home
Part of broken marriage,
Thinking about removing broken
Stone from his broken shoe,
Repairing the broken statue
That he carries.

Looking left then right
Then back again;
Not knowing which way to go,
He was taught not to leap
Into this crossing.
But if he had looked he would
Have seen the possibilities
Stretching out like
An endless dream

And while sleeping policemen
Give him a nod and
Forty blinkered winks
He thinks that his breath,
White and caught in the air's cold clutch,
Could turn the red to pink.

His amber-gambler once wife depressed,
At the seven horses that left her
Bereft of gogo ge-ge fever,
Not the ones that made her the winner,
The Ascot hat of the disco diva.

And so when these lights will
Turn to green
And cars will pass in a careless stream,
He will see the chance that was to be taken
Now
Gone;
And in a one-way street will continue on.

Hecate's Silver

"Is the moon gonna
   shine all night, Chap?"
      The Suitcases, Anne Hall Whitt

It is the silver of a heart,
The clawing of a paw
And the wolf I do not fear
As he stalks me
With his feet on fire.
Tonight will burn all nights
Known to us in a chance
Of lost promises made before
He sucked the blood dry
From her bones, spitting them
Like Jack sprat.
Books you read as children
Were pornography in disguise,
Red Riding Hood was full of
Want for her wolf,
But who would do it in their
Grandmother's bed?
With guilt of an angry heart
And shame of an imaginative mind.
Princes of poetry and
Their Newcastle tongues
Sound louder in the dark,
4am, moon still shining
Aglow on silence, a stage bow,
A final whisper as the entertainer
Juggles with stars.

I love magic and witchcraft,
And I love the sound of sleeplessness
As it winds through telephone wires
Into a dumbness and desert of
Cracked sand heart attacks.

If the moon shines all night
Then ghosties will play
And four legged beasties will
Bare fangs that sound of iron
And the grass is always greener
In the graveyard.
Give me a wolf and his howl.
Give me silver and sorcery.
Give me the heart of a magus man
Whose tongue will speak in spells.
Give me an itch that satisfies the
Scratch in a wild wolf woman's
 Amber eyes on barbed wire fighting.

Where is the scream that became stuck
In the throat of a murderer's wife
As she flicked the knife and tongued
The gun and slept in bed with
The butcher's son who dreamt
Of grazing cattle jumping a bleeding moon.
Hey diddle diddle let's all have a fiddle
Because the baby has swallowed its spoon.

The moon it shone all night, chaps,
The moon it shone all night,
The ghosties didn't come,
Four legged beasties lay latent
In their shadows,
And the murdered woman,
The murdered woman,
Was silent.

Sexy Anne's Plan

Sexy Anne had a plan,
That sexy Anne would get a man,
And for this plan of sexy Anne's
Sexy Anne would need to find that man;
Sexy Anne had this circus stand.

Here, every rat truly was a star.
Fantastic acrobatics had antics with
fanatics drunk on Frascati.
Breathing in the deepness
Of her Big Top Tent

Sexy Anne would take
The circus stand
And so to speak to every man
And tell them of
The sexy Anne plan.

Sexy Anne sizzled
In the drizzle,
Sexy Anne was in the middle
Of a real quizzical fiddle;
She spat and shined her shoes.

Sexy Anne swarmed with silver
And lured with looks of
Glinting winking lead in
The bed cred.
Sexy Anne spurned the women.

Sexy Anne sent then swimming
With thoughts of the man plan
The kick-crotch high can-can.
The lips of sexy Anne
Smoked.

Sexy Anne would snatch a man
With a tightness dreamed
By devils – the level would bevel
And the playing field flood.
Sexy Anne shimmered.

Super slick Sexy Anne
Got her man:
The fiddle unriddled
And god the girl sizzled:
Her tongue flicked his sex sharp grizzle.

Sexy Anne took the circus stand
And marched off merry
With her man in hand
Her stomach to her knees tanned.

Love letters

Alpha was the one,
Though he did not have the bravado of Charlie
Who was the first I ever kissed,
In a cubicle where we could hear the pissing
Of the girl next door.

We would drive to the river's delta
And hear the children's playground echo
They that life had yet to helter-skelter,
And how we learned to know the ways in which
A fox could trot in the back of that battered Golf. GTI.

One time in foolish anticipation of what we could be
We drove to a hotel where the curtains were
Indigo blue and booked a room with a seaview
And a balcony that was four from above to below
And there outside he stood and shouted

"Juliet". And we never even spent the night.
Instead we laughed at the fisherman with their old wives
Tales and bought a kilo of their catch which we cracked
Into one another's mouths as we planned to steal a boat and
Sail to Lima. Then I met Mike.

It was a November and the fog made orange circle swirls
As it breathed the morning's newness. He had an Oscar-winning
Film star grin and hummed the words To "Papa was a rolling stone."
His pool-cue-beckoned me over, though I nearly missed it
Through the smoke that snaked him.

He was no Romeo, you understand. It was quick
And careless in the passenger seat of his Dad's Sierra,
I watched the mountains bob in-and-out of view over
His shoulder and thought of how my grandmother was
Tangoed by a man in uniform before ending here.

Then there was my victor, he was whiskey drinking, wining
Dining, hard loving, fast driving, crazy talking,
Always smoking, motor bike riding, with a lamppost colliding,
Police were hiding, he was running and running with his
Broken head and at the hospital somebody read his x-ray wrong.
Gone.

There was a funeral, flowers, six black horses and all hells angels
saluted.
Some schoolboy pact was kept and Yankee Doodle sung. The service
was strange
And his parents travelled from Africa with a language I knew not of,
"Zulu", said an angel with the letter 'A' written upon his back and
hair all long
And that's how I came to know that Alpha was one.

ABIGAIL OBORNE

Abigail Oborne writes poetry, prose, plays and screenplays. She is currently studying in Putney, London and is recently married. Before university she worked for a charity based on a high-rise council estate in London. Her main role was to help isolated elderly people make friends and to keep children and young people out of trouble. Abigail's writing is influenced by a wide range of influences. She's currently enjoying the poems of Gertrude Stein, Tom Raworth and Frank O'Hara, the songs of Rufus Wainwright and the visual art of David Shrigley and Banksy.

suffering

when the Tsunami
two hundred thousand people
my wife's mother

eight days later we heard that she'd died
getting the chicken
her father dropped down dead

huge shock
as a family
buildings collapse into the ground

seventy five thousand died
young boys go for a walk
bang

kills him
bang
just coz he's black

and all of these things
when we live in a suffering
in a painful world

Kid

Yeah so I
wiped coffee froth off my
wrists and watched
the cars and plastic bags
sifting past the window
heard the man say "I'm so excited
I'm just so excited about my fifteen
pound saving on my iPod-digi-nodal-modal-camera-lover"
and pick up his

blinking child. Listen kid,
I don't know what
kind of world has welcomed you
but still I sit here
cappuccino fed and biscotti wrapper
dead shell. Still the buses, the buses
coming fast, three in each direction
but here's a solid silence between you

and me, the best thing
between all my crappy jobs
and angry days.
"It's you and me babe,"
I heard you say at seven thirty
this morning over the hairdryer and the
clang of my
eyes
so here's today and it's you and
me babe/mate/brother/sister/dad/God.

Poems

of a slag and other things
like
and poems as if i was ever
with my life and I do
plenty of
I'm sick of like,
listening to
but sorry's a funny word
stop being such a retard
or
in the here and now and
getting sick of whinging
getting
in the lounge for hours
singing
dried chords shit I have a
voice
says nothing but blahblah
and
blah and I've got all
kinds of
a dirty wallet and a
loyalty card
wasn't Nero the geezer
that
and fed them all to the
lions?

sonnet no.3

when I say I love you
it sounds like the flip
of a cheque book or
sneeze or
c o u g h
maybe a car
horn or egg
h u r l e d
but it's only language
could've said it
washing the dishes or
writing a letter
but I said it today at 2:34
after I'd eaten a sandwich.

sonnet no.11

quarter to two time
too twisted to twingle now
thrice discarded and reheated
eaten or left to stand for two
minutes before serving your
community in an apron makers
kitchen cupboard love baby an'
write me a sonnet bout livin on a
council estate concrete land of
opportunity next to big city
dwellers in bigger cars or carrot
soup in organick paper cups an
it's called carrot and coriander
broth wiv added vitamin we. Ha!

sonnet no.13

sifting days, weeks, hours
rubbing your mind along the
shifting jerking along looking
you spoke to me and I listened
were going and I knew how it
you think I didn't tell you think
I or cry when you think I didn't
on the floorboards till dawn or
shut myself away with you? with
you for hours nights weeks say
you wanted to come back be with
me for it to be over but over today
and we walked and you cried
looking at the gravestones

The World

The world gets darker now.
November and 5:14 p.m.
and it seems
everything has been rubbed out,

apart from those windows;
bedroom, office, kitchen,
the only slabs of light. Listen.
Mute arguments, jokes, confessions,

sirens,
planes that ache and sigh across this sky.
I watched 'Macbeth' and turned it off,
drank hot choclate, then watched

someone I didn't know open a door
and empty a mop bucket into the ground.
I think you should know
even in this November, even in this night,

that you are more
than a player, have more
than an hour, can do more than fret upon this stage.
That, for the price of a ticket, you can slide

blinking over this sky. That you can buy
with the coins in your pocket, a paper cup of chocolate,
hold it till your fingers blush and grow
a little fatter, a little warmer in this night.

coz I'm Questioning that how he answers the phone anymore, just this anonymous, just this hello. Hello? And I wasn't sure whether she was, whether she even was anymore. Not "Hello, Tina speaking" or "Hello Tina's house." Questioning that 'hello' should even be a question at all. Shouldn't there be?

yeah No. Yeah. Sorry. Yeah. Rubbish. Yeah. You'd said it was rubbish. Yeah.

thinking Why? So. That's. So. Didn't? So. That's. So. That's. It really. Look, I think. I *am* bloody. I don't want you to. What? So you can. Don't be so. There's some more. Yes please. In the pot. *She pours some more tea.*

about everything Looking in clucking bins trucking tins made of things shade of cringe about fringe about fringe about the fringe of things about singe about the singe of things looking in bins looking at trucking looking with tins shade under bins shade on the fringe on the fringe of things clucking in tins in the tins of things of things made of shade made of shade and tins from the fringe on the fringe looking for cringes looking for singes and clucking and clucking at clucking still clucking or trucking back trucking of trucking to the fridge of things to the fringe of things of things made of tins of things of things of things made of tins and everything else and everything else and everything else like that.

like drinking the elderly hoping for style and bought it hoping for dingy Oxbridge formal halls or the more affordable versions you might find on a bistro menu or the kitchens of the working class but none the less there are rules like an earlier said style like an ironic mullet like world camp and London geezer like a quietly chuffed haircut amongst a few beers and as many salacious stories and there's a part of me there's a part of me that would love to tell you would love to tell you mate

how O Lord *She stirs the* your servants mercifully and thanksgiving thee to grant Jesus Christ and all thy of our sins, And Sugar? Through slavery, giving him, you raised, you exalted and people love problems. Here Lord, ourselves reasonable humbly partakers and in the paper there are lives and fulfilled with benediction through any sacrifice or aren't you sweet enough? our bounden merits Jesus Christ whom, in honour and almighty. Therefore, and with we proclaim for ever. Holy, holy, God of heaven and Hosanna and anonymous office building. Coz we take special books of problems to bed with us, polishing off a moderate sudoku with a

Sunday Ten to Three

It's Sunday ten to three at Steve's
everyone's out buying milk or
something for lunch and I've been entertaining
passing visitors with year old stories of
drunkenness.
Outside, a Sunday sky;
no rain, no sun, just sludges
of grey and blue and birds
draped on indecisive trees.

But the motivated are running
near the river, couples with matching tracksuits
ice white iPods bouncing off their chests
while the refined frown at papers, thinking
they hold the 'long and short of it' all
in the pages between blackening fingers.

But here I'm consoled
by a silence or an absence
of words, just a tapping
of laptops and the clangs and rustles
and bursts of running water
from Steve making lunch downstairs.

Further though;
the soft and constant yapping
of dogs
at nothing much
on the next street.

Nearer
next door, just audible
warbled hymns on an out-of-tune organ
from the elderly at church.

JAMES WILKES

Born in Dorset in 1980, James studied Psychology and Philosophy before taking an MA in Creative Writing at UEA. After a year teaching and working on organic farms in Japan, he published *Ex Chaos* (Renscombe Press, 2006), poems based on Japanese creation myths. He has read on BBC Radio 4, exhibited poem-objects including papier-mâché bowls and modified egg boxes, and contributed to *Studio International*, *Terrible Work* and *Intercapillary Space*. His most recent publication is *A DeTour*, a series of hand-printed postcards that rework selections from Daniel Defoe's *A Tour thro' the Whole Island of Great Britain*.

Ex Chaos

SHHIIIIIIIIIINNN

indicates silence, speech's term for its own absence,
the unspeakable bustle
rising through the limen of language.

The world is like floating oil, or a jellyfish,
or black as lily seeds, or lamp black.
Before this was no force or form
incised scraped traced rubbed sanded,
nought done nought named
in graphite, tool, or ochre with vermilion
to fix the greedy spread by layering up or gouging or topography –

No waves form light sound or pond ripples
No light force push particles to leap –

So how do I know? *By trusting the former sages.*

Score for a Nocturne

the   hissing   electric   loops
night

             wheels   benison
                      non-stop   like
cantata   of   night

of   neon   loom   like
patched   black   and   film
mirrors   /

                      pass   and
passing
             sulphur   of   empty
city   escape

                                  except
cinematic   this
lighthouse of
             rain   samples
             alleys

swept   signs   signals
past

                      buried
                      arteries   one
                                  noir
                      metropolis

                                vehicle

Untitled

"Tyde flowing is feared for many a thing,
Great danger to such as be sick it doth bring"
    Thomas Tusser, *Five Hundred Points of Good Husbandrie* (1557)

"Battler Diane was denied a peaceful end"
    Overseen newspaper headline

Mechanical ebb clicks to flood,
the heating. The pipes rinse, squeak,
gurgle; they enjoy routine.

The pipes run still and deep,
Diane the Battler perspires. She is battling,
all her names allow.

A woodline, moon's woodcut
high tide. Her owl steers a perfect wake
jumps fully armed to mouse-noise

in the pipes. Diane awake, feels surrender
waving white flags, I'll leave these names
now, clothes on the floor.

Denied. Diane you are a battler
call the pipes. Sweat in the sick shop,
great danger. Moon rips pipes from walls.

A Postcard from the New Forest

NEW FOREST in *Hampshire* was singled out to be the place

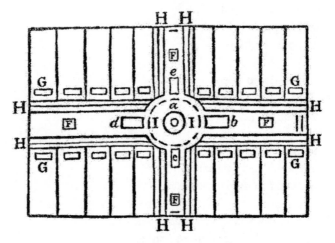

Propos'd Re-peopling thus:

a The absolute Weavers of equal Spring
b Calculation of Shambles to Cure the Land
c People *gratis* to circulating Butter
d True born Shoemakers, handsome Plumbers
e Three Acres of Parish Barbers here
F Fenc'd, Plow'd, Sow'd: This is Corporation Bacon
G A Wind-Mill, a Wheel-Barrow, a Stranger
H Necessarily and voluntarily, Physicians out the Forest
I Painters to Teach all to Speak

A Postcard from Rochester

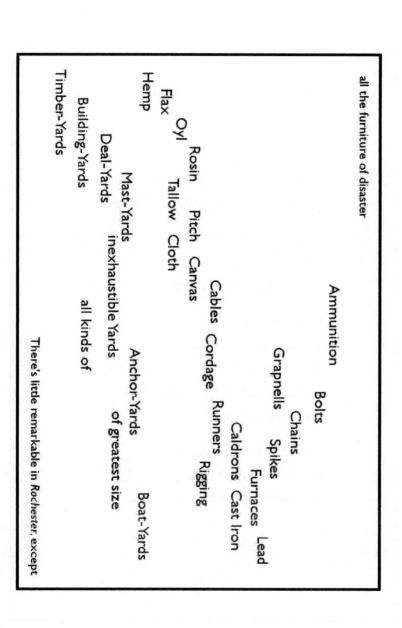

all the furniture of disaster

Ammunition

Bolts

Chains

Grapnells   Spikes

Furnaces   Lead

Caldrons Cast Iron

Hemp
Flax

Oyl   Rosin   Pitch   Canvas

Tallow   Cloth

Cables Cordage Runners

Rigging

Mast-Yards
Deal-Yards   inexhaustible Yards   Anchor-Yards   Boat-Yards

of greatest size

Building-Yards   all kinds of

Timber-Yards

There's little remarkable in *Rochester*, except

A Postcard from the Isle of Purbeck

Miles we flew in view of the Sea
Quantities of Shipping and Rocks

vast Quarreys of Herbage
sweet as Stone
Grey, Red, Black, and other Colours

an Eagle like the Wind
so strong so outrageous
fine to an extream but too strong
it bit him and beat him
with Velvet Wings

an open Peice of Ground
the fine Carpet Ground
sweet as Herbs soft as Velvet

A Postcard from Eldon Hole

In an open Field
gently descending to South
is a frightful Imagination
or opening in the Earth

    It goes down perpendicular

Two Villains led a Traveller
to the Edge of this Gulph
and bad him take a large step;

    He stept at once into Eternity

What Nature meant in leaving
its Window open, I cannot tell

Tea

"A little Tea one leaf I did not steal
For Guiltless Blood shed I to GOD appeal
Put Tea in one scale human Blood in tother
And think what tis to slay thy harmless Brother"
    From the gravestone of Robert Trotman, shot whilst smuggling tea 1765

1

Knotted to a thread of sand
a vicious affair in the dark knives out
the felt pack-horses, squeal and tumble.
A squalid local spat enough for death
inserts its old lever, lays you
tangled on your back never to randy
no more, trudge, or take pleasure.
I see you, Robert Trotman with
black tea running from your sinking
its black spikes in the slurry
of wet sand – drifts against your face
its fine monumental scent.

I will force myself to drink
not monster not martyr your eyes.
The parson's blessing to risk pain and deal it,
was it seized or bestowed?
You say nothing – a wind stirs
the reedbeds. To wash with sea water
the posed piety of epitaph
through channeled sand, the
soft astringency of tea shifting
wordlessly with woodsmoke
must come closer. I cannot even
see your eyes, through all this.

2

Two eyes will sleep no more.
Excised of failings with a sharp knife
Bodhidharma's eyelids are cast leaves
garnished with flowers as of sweet-brier
"and like in bigness, but of smell unlike".
The long reach of waters blow
black fuses home, curled tips of waves.
In Bihar a single leaf, they say
fell unerringly to a ring of water,
cool inward bell of it –
but already the clippers cut across
with unbound greed, the royal love, i.e.

"all sorts of rarities and rich goods
fit for my palace" of nauseating marble,
the maps crossed with cannon-smoke
a mercantile projection. This black trail
leads half-way round the world, its couriers
considered ants, as Bodhidharma pitied.
One, broken by the unseen touch
of taper to fuse, and being alive,
screamed to the end of a
tangled brocade, of pain and desire
over vast emptiness, empires,
kettle steam, sand.

3

Prokudin-Gorskii, photographer to the Tsar
to empires of lives and their collapse
recorded in startling colour a moment
of Greek women picking tea –
skirts and headscarves and the challenge of eyes
over undiscovered graves – the Black Sea coast –
a buried Greco-Colchian settlement.

Tea bushes, brambles, sand, the sky's
silt bay – the sensual archeology
of things,
                    a vast anchor.

Being sat in a warm grave
living skin pulvered with the long dead
and feel in my fingers where
the collars dovetailed down:
intimacy of a kind
history cannot pierce,
its streamered narratives.

Caught eddies gather slow hours,
clouds. The ordered rows are tangling
in late summer, to a bramble ripeness
this "Post-Soviet" now.

4 variations on the same midwinter

1

The gold cover and
the world breathing birth to zero.
The weather bleached of haunt.
It's now love, to decline.

2

Breath witness
of hare's haunt, and sheep's.
Fire now. Light me.
Don't dim beside day.

3

Light's lower rip to curtain
so I stood breathing the weather of hare and sheep.
If ever it's still, inquisitive and bright.

4

Through eve, so
birth the barrow the fields.
Un-flowered on blether
need roused fingers and rise
brimming.

Wild Flowers of Britain and Europe

Split wood handles or
Hare-lipped babies on hillsides
Exposed mean nothing to me, I like to
Enter illegally, roar through the unlicensed
Parties. Reuse the dag-ends and snip the badgers'
Scrag. Countryside's only good for
Burning onions, anyway, cover it
In slush of brine and
Teleport the inhabitants to Saudi.

Forensics labs are a sort
Of playground too, chemical A
Xylene plus any Alkaloid gives a good hit,
Good crack. Plaque removal no prob neither,
Lever your teeth out with plurals.
Over my dead body eggheads chant,
Varicose stats are mere as venison,
Elegant but done rarely.

Sprach and sprite commonly
Elope these mountaintops almost
Almeida or southern in their hunger,
Lapis lazuli colouring the hare's eye.
Apes invested with string theory,
Violently drunk on parallel grams of
Entropy. Where did real science go?
Nailing sheep in the genome field
Despair of their mothers, these butchers
Estranged the left but left the
Royalties untouched.

Wordsworth pondered the balance of
Illegalities and plumped for the paycheque.
Laissez-faire works for yokels and inbred
Dilettantes, he muttered, but O fat-head
Masters, where's the donkey's arse going if

Any Philip with a 2-2 in gene therapy can
Dance the innumerables with happy cheer?
Data wrecked the speedboat!
Eat happy for long but don't best the
Rats if you want to see tomorrow.